ISBN: 978-1-989832-04-2
Copyright 2021 EcoPembroke. EcoPembroke@gmail.com

Studio Dreamshare Press
Pembroke, Ontario, Canada
www.studiodreamsharepress.com
Inquiries: publishing@studiodreamshare.com

Table of Contents

Focus of this PhotoVoice Project: "Glimpses of Tomorrow"

Youth artists in our community met with adults to create an intergenerational dialogue about patterns and visions of environmental sustainability and climate change experienced and seen in their everyday lives in our community. We spent a week at Studio Dreamshare in summer 2021 engaging in conversations, sharing art, and inspiring and supporting one another to create the pieces that make up this exhibition.

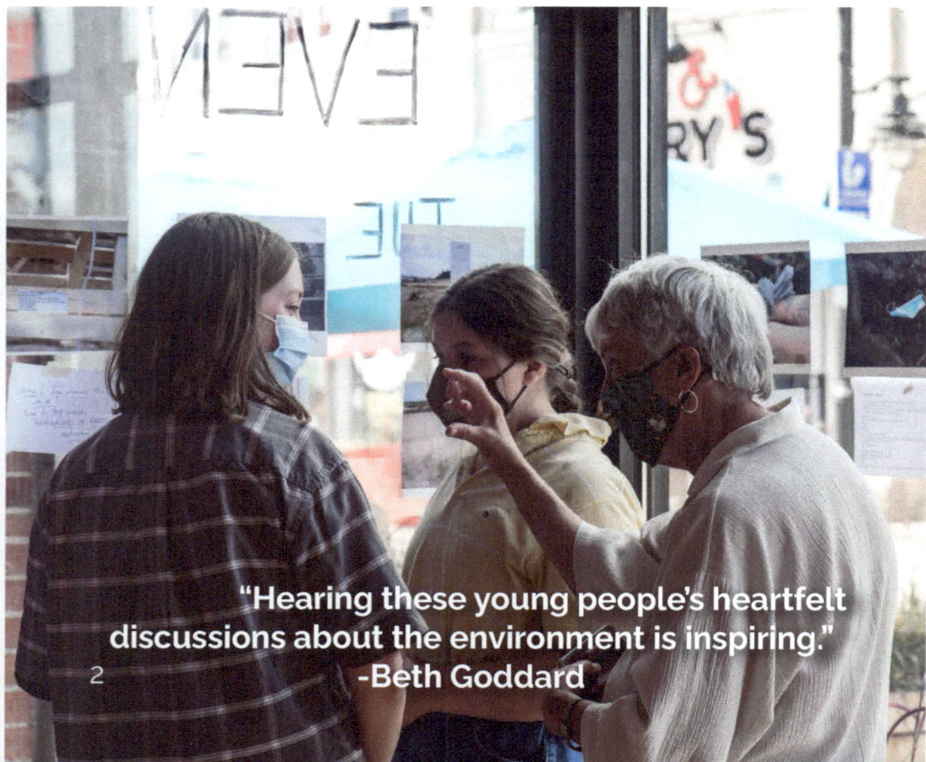

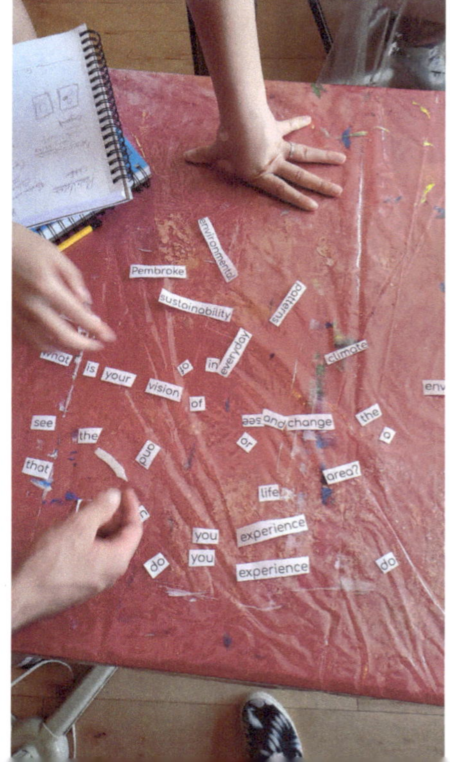

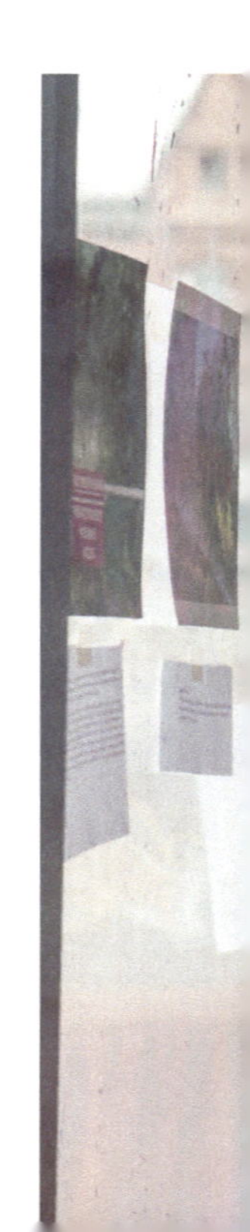

Photovoice Ottawa Valley 2021

What is PhotoVoice? A method where group participants use pictures to focus their experiences and thoughts about an issue that is overlooked and in need of awareness in the whole community. Working together, the group's visual statements become a powerful communication tool for advocating change. Core Belief: That people of the community itself, not outside experts, are in the best position to understand the strengths and limitations of their own community to undertake such social change.

Exhibition Statement

The worse the state of the planet,

The more helpless we feel.

If we start to fix it,

It will get better.

Responsibility is tied to the common good.

Entrapment—trapped by our own mistakes.

Resiliency.

Justice.

Redemption is earned through action.

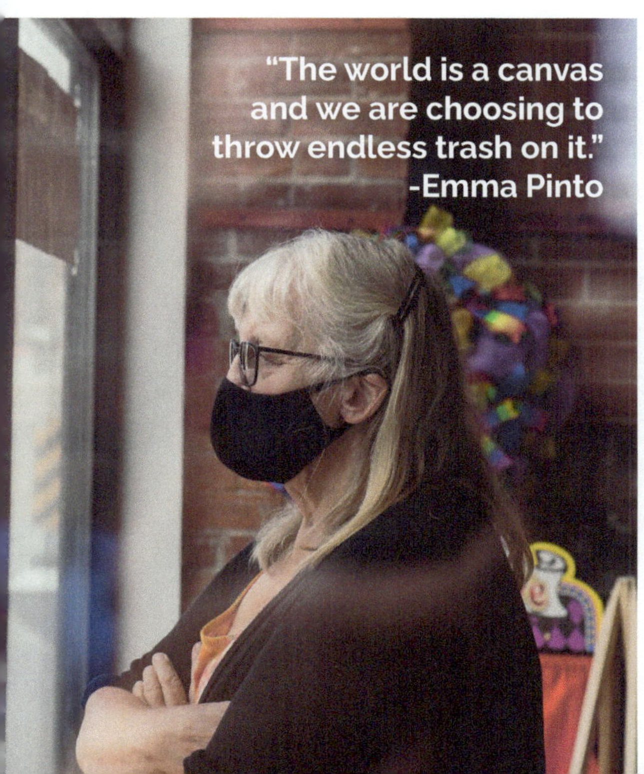

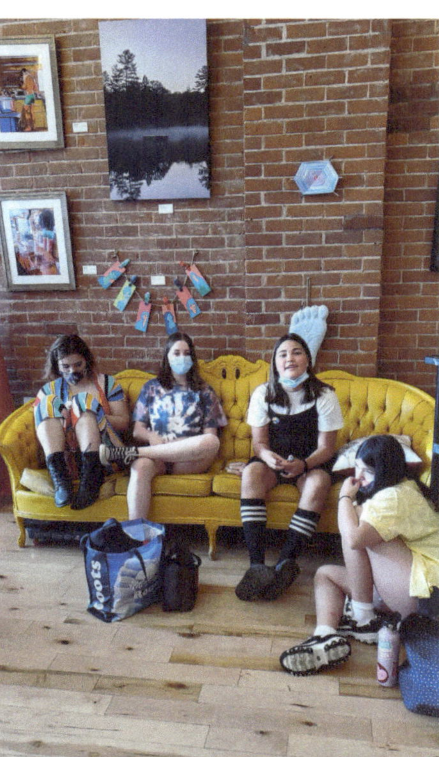

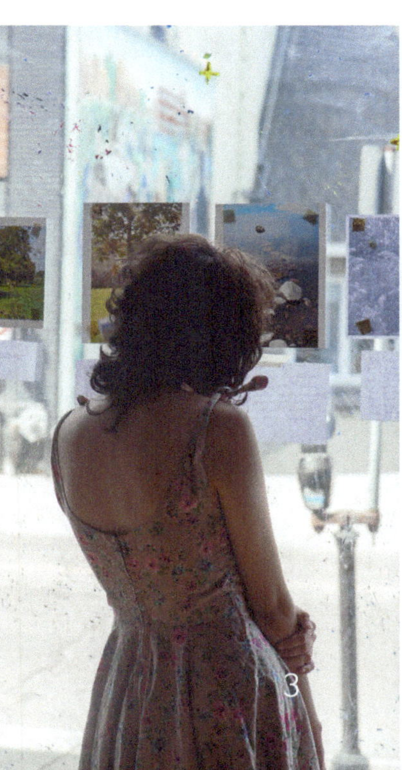

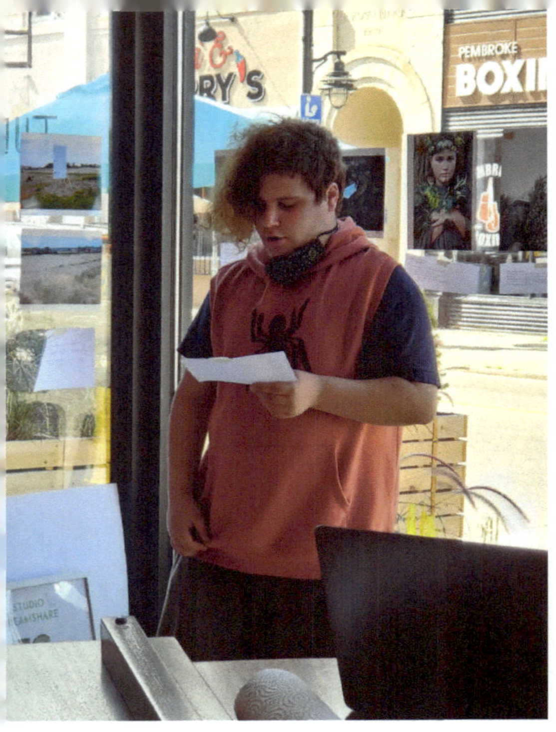

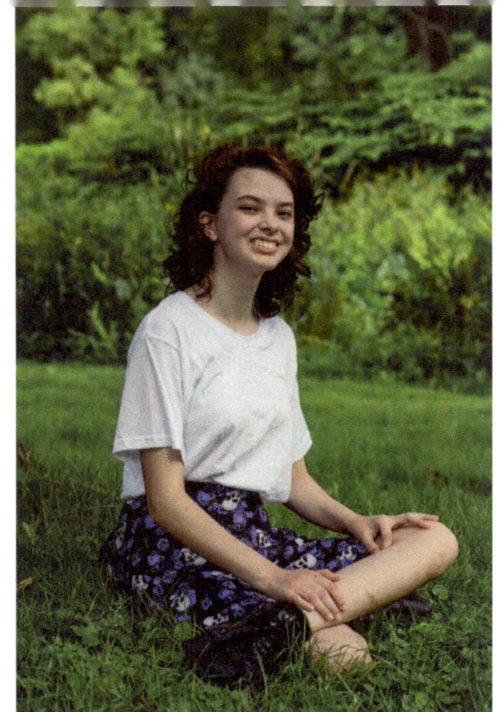

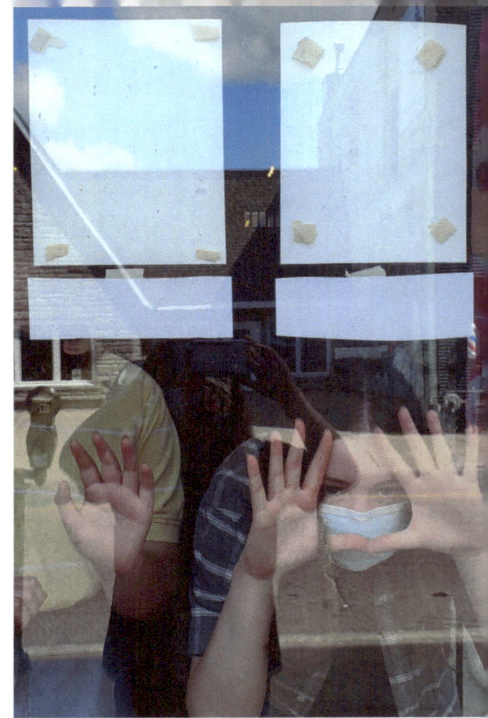

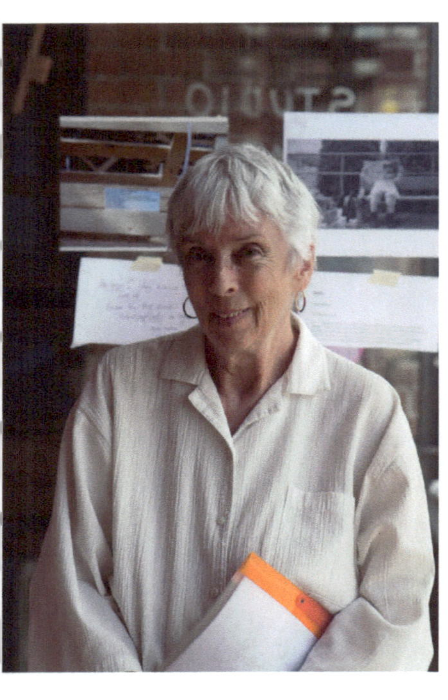

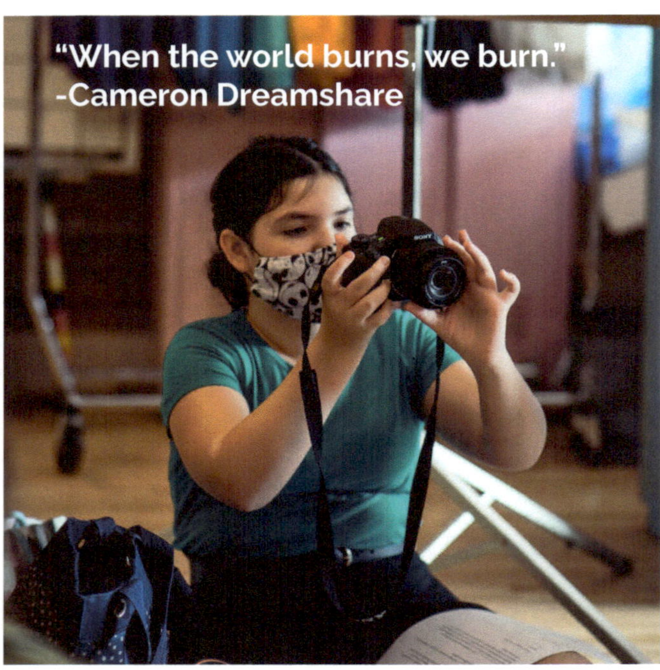

"When the world burns, we burn."
-Cameron Dreamshare

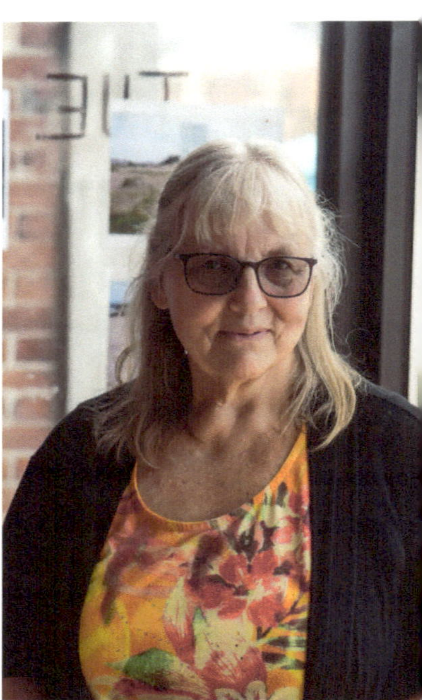

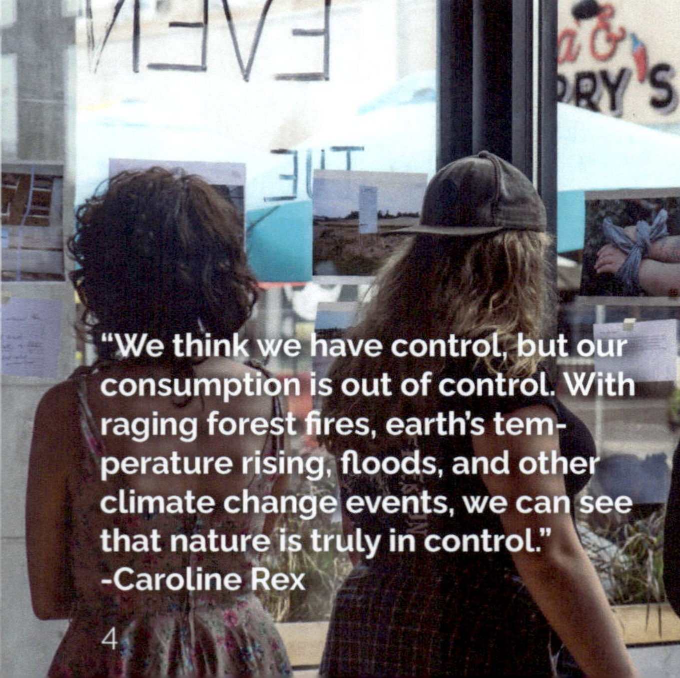

"We think we have control, but our consumption is out of control. With raging forest fires, earth's temperature rising, floods, and other climate change events, we can see that nature is truly in control."
-Caroline Rex

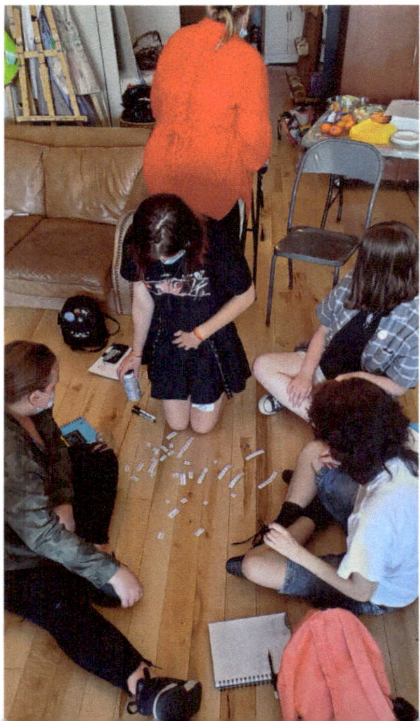

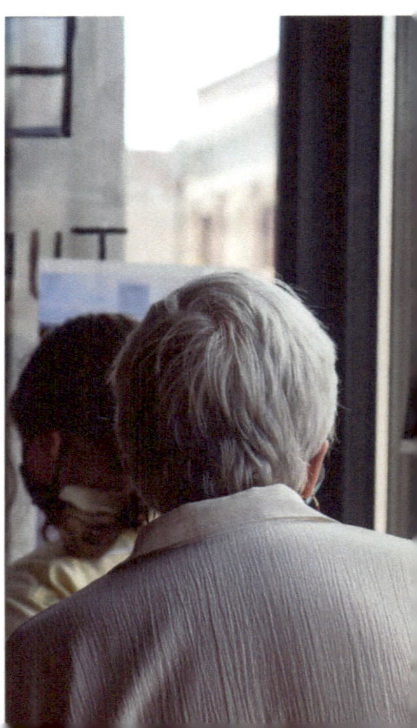

A Note From Rev. Tiina Cote

Greetings and Welcome to the experience that will unfold on these pages!

Where does a vision come from to gather an intergenerational group to ponder and photograph their insights of the interaction between humanity and the natural world? It started 3 years ago with Greta Thunberg, a girl who spoke at the United Nations about climate change, condemning world leaders for failing to act. A year later, back in Canada, a teen water warrior demanded that the Prime Minister commit to ensuring clean drinking water on all First Nations Territories. A few months later, Pembroke and area youth joined others in holding Fridays-for-Future rallies in downtown Pembroke. These rallies brought attention to the climate catastrophe which will unfold in the life time of those teens and young adults unless we move into radical changes now.

In 2020, EcoPembroke began planning ways to engage our community in conversation and action related to local environmental challenges and climate change. The catalyst for this Photovoice project was the unique activism we saw in Greta Thunberg at the UN, the Canadian challenge to our Prime Minister for safe drinking water, and the Fridays-for-Future activism. It stimulated a vision of capturing through photography the feelings and thoughts of individuals from several generations, showing their hopes and challenges regarding today's and tomorrow's interactions between humanity and the natural world.

"Glimpses of Tomorrow" was born. It is a Photovoice project that gives an empowering framework to youth, young adults and seniors as they share with others their personal insights and feelings around these complex issues. Some used the camera to document local situations; and others, more general interactions between humanity and the natural world. The photographs and the stories you will see in this publication are profound and humbling. They are definitely poised to foster dialogue and action to change our world.

Thank you to each participant and to the community partners, especially Studio Dreamshare, for sharing your voices and creativity. As we engage in this wider conversation about human life on planet earth, may the thread of unique climate activism keep growing. Together we will bring positive change for a better future.

With thanks for the generous funding support from the Eastern Ontario and Outaouais Region and Calvin/ Wesley United Churches, along with community partners EcoPembroke and Studio Dreamshare.

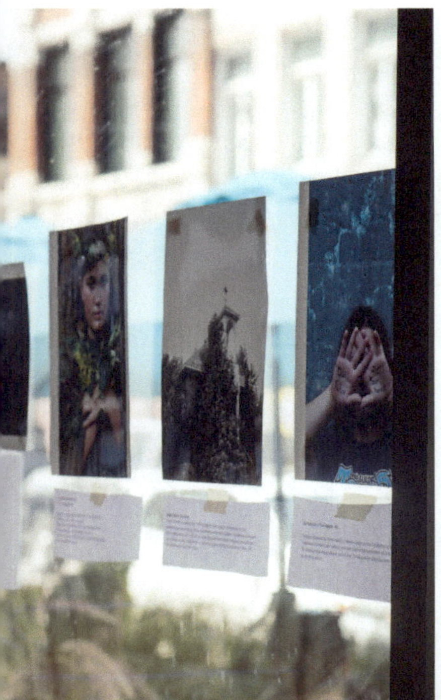

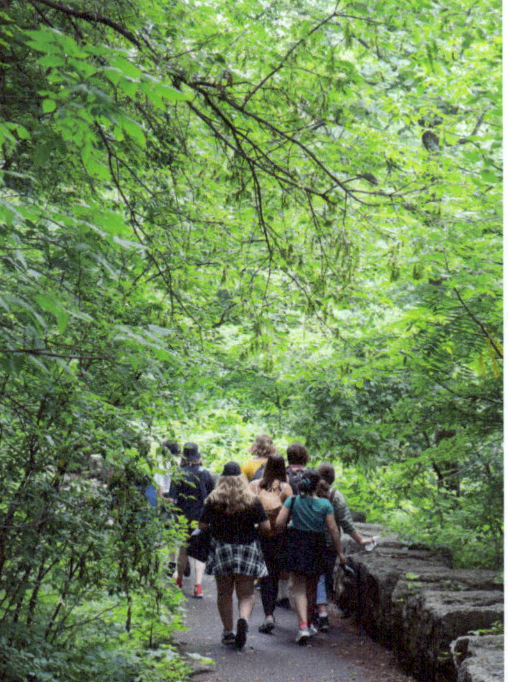

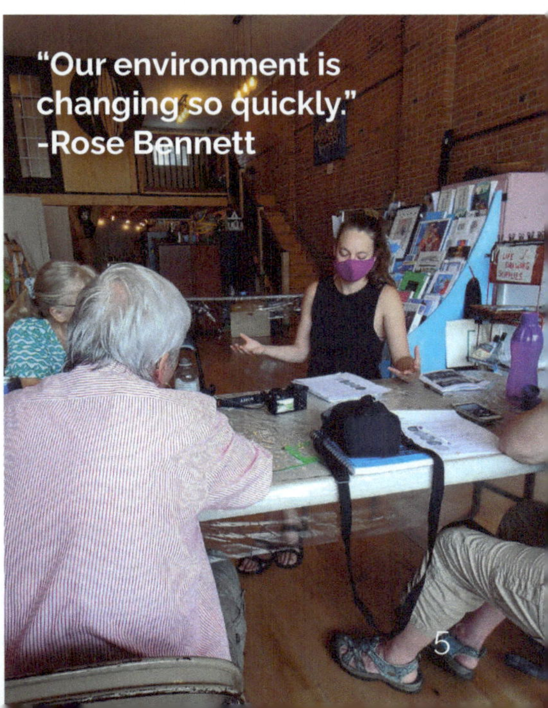

How to Use Art as a Tool for Environmental Activism

By Tys Burger

For a while now I've been aware of the climate crisis as one of the most important issues of our time. As a kid, my school would pick up trash on the side of the road once a year for Earth Week. As I got a bit older and entered high-school, I came to understand pollution and the degradation of the planet as a more complex issue. I learned about carbon emissions from burning fossil fuels which contribute to raising the planet's average temperature, and I learned about the interdependence of ecosystems and how when one part of the earth is affected it has rippling consequences.

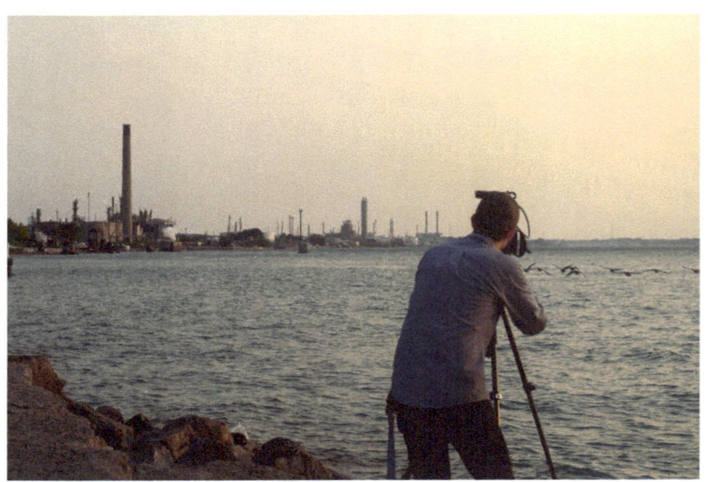

I learned about giant industries that mine huge amounts of the earth's resources to be made into everything that we know and recognize: the wood that my house is made of contributes to defor-estation; my car emits toxic emissions; and all of the plastics, paints, soaps, tires, make-up ink and basically everything else that makes my way of life possible are made from crude oil--the extract-ing and refining of which are incredibly harmful to the earth (not to mention that many of these products have an almost infinite lifespan).

Gradually, an image was beginning to form in my mind of a large, impenetrable system, rotten inside and out and immune to any protest. It left me feeling discouraged and paralysed, and like the problem was far too big and convoluted for me to have any kind of voice or positive impact.

Many people I've met share some version of this feeling of apathy. But there is another kind of environmental awareness that I've recognized in our society too, which is one where environmental issues are restricted entirely to the realm of personal responsibility. Some people find a lot of motivation to lessen their own carbon footprint by pursuing the difficult yet noble task of elimi-nating single-use plastics from their lives, biking or walking to places when possible, living within their means. But when I think of people taking the full weight of the climate emergency onto their own shoulders, it reminds me of the British Petroleum commercial from the year 2000, which is where the term "carbon footprint" was first coined. This multinational petroleum producer, BP, ran a public ad campaign to shift the blame for fossil fuel emissions and the pollution of our planet from big oil companies onto consumers, and it was really effective.

Now, I don't want to suggest that individual responsibility is unimportant--a society is made up of individuals, after all. But the sins of pollution are not committed equally. The richest 10% of people in the world account for 50% of our global emissions, according to a report by Oxfam. And not only that, but the poorest people are then the ones who see the worst consequences: Poor and racial-ized groups experience the highest levels of air pollution--and suffer greater health impacts and even premature death because of it--and those groups are also disproportionately exposed to disasters like droughts, floods and heat waves.

I strive to be more like my friends and neighbours who are committed to reducing their personal footprint on the environment, but I also don't want to lose sight of the economic system that we live in, and the inequality that is so closely tied with the climate issues that are raised.

A good quote I heard about climate activism recently was "I used to think the top environmental problems were biodiversity loss, ecosystem collapse and climate change. I thought that with 30 years of good science we could address these problems. But I was wrong. The top environmental problems are selfishness, greed and apathy, and to deal with those we need a spiritual and cultural transformation, and we scientists don't know how to do that," spoken by Gus Speth, a climate activist and lawyer.

Tackling the climate emergency solely in my own life felt futile without also trying to contribute to the cultural transformation called for by Gus Speth. And then it struck me that art is a realm where I can engage with some of the broader and more complex (and systemic) problems associated with climate change. That led me to begin a film project called Petrolia, which is a feature-length documentary centering the history of oil extraction in Canada. The film begins in the town of Petrolia, where oil was first struck in Canada, and eventually makes its way to Alberta to see where the industry is at now, all while centering First Nations' perspectives, and comparing their relationship to land to the colonial relationship that settlers imposed here. It will also explore the changes that oil has contributed to our lives, for good and for bad, and ultimately make the call for a reduced dependency on the substance and a shift towards a more responsible use of resources in society.

For me, making Petrolia feels like an active way to talk about the system we're in, and to bring people's attention to the oil executives making plastics and other (over 6000!) oil-based products. While the project is only just starting, my hope for the film is to clarify what the core issues of the climate emergency really are, so that people can be better equipped to tackle them.

After I returned from my first trip to Petrolia, photovoice week began, and I couldn't think of a better time for me to be considering and discussing the connection between art and environmental activism. I applaud all of the artists in the show, and encourage them, and the people viewing the show, to continue to explore art as a tool that can ask powerful questions and start the kinds of conversations that motivate people towards protest, voting and any other tools for change that come available.

For updates on Petrolia through production you can follow the page Elytra Collective on Facebook.

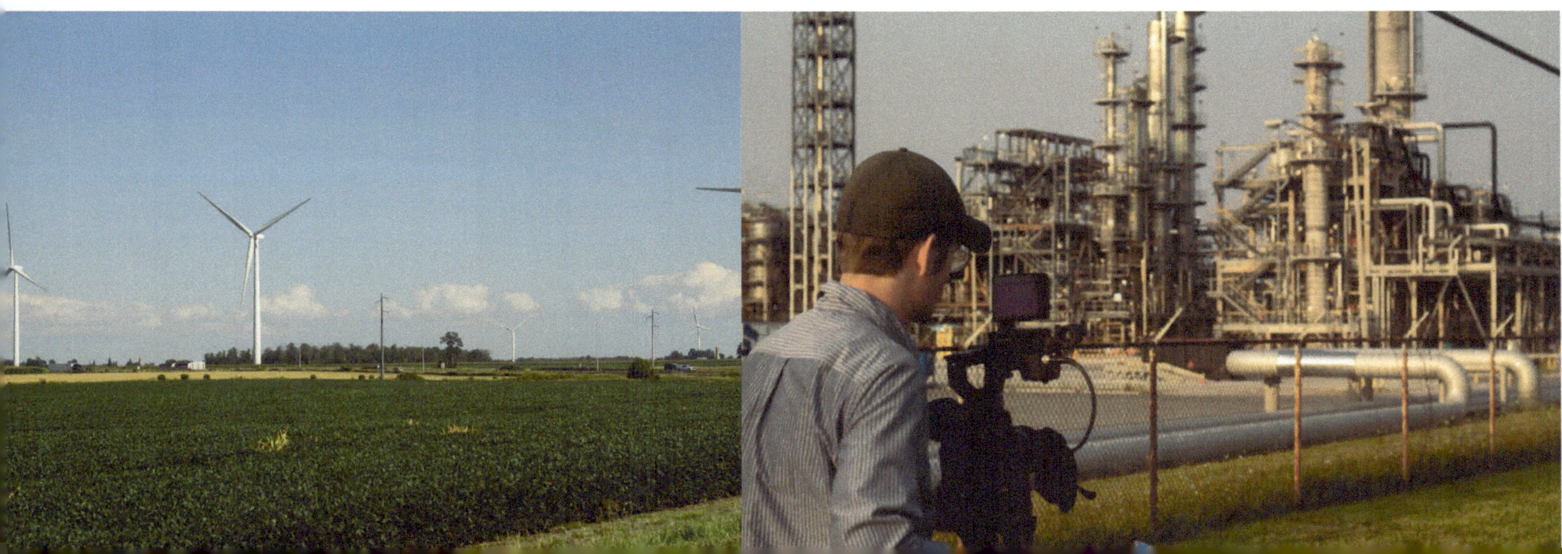

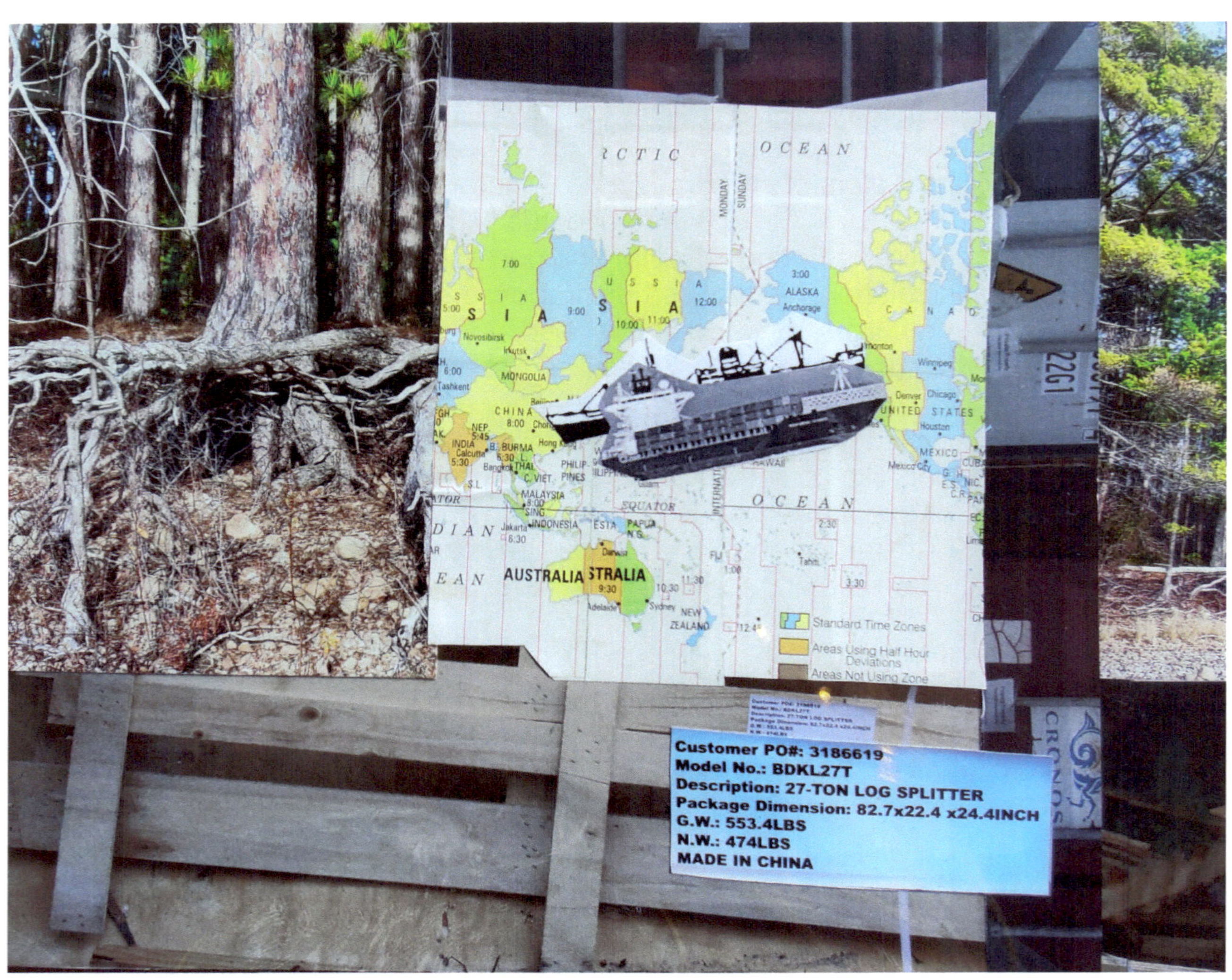

Sustainability, Beth Goddard, mixed-media collage, 2021.

Sustainability

by Beth Goddard

Making a collage that speaks to the issue of climate change is a challenge. I started by finding the labelled pallets in the garbage set out behind a local shopping mall. The connection with China is very evident and the product purchased from China is a 'log splitter'; something used by loggers as a part of the trade of wood, a natural product that Canada sells world-wide. But is it possible that Canada originally sold the wood to China? Certainly machinery was housed in the wooden pallets for its trip from China to the store of the local mall. Does that mean the wood crossed the Pacific Ocean and most of the width of Canada, perhaps twice? Think of the shipping costs. Why is Canada not producing its own machinery? Consider the effect of such trade on current ecological sources. The photos of trees suffering from the diminishing water levels in the closest source of hydration is painful. Is Canada really taking care of its forests today? Just think...

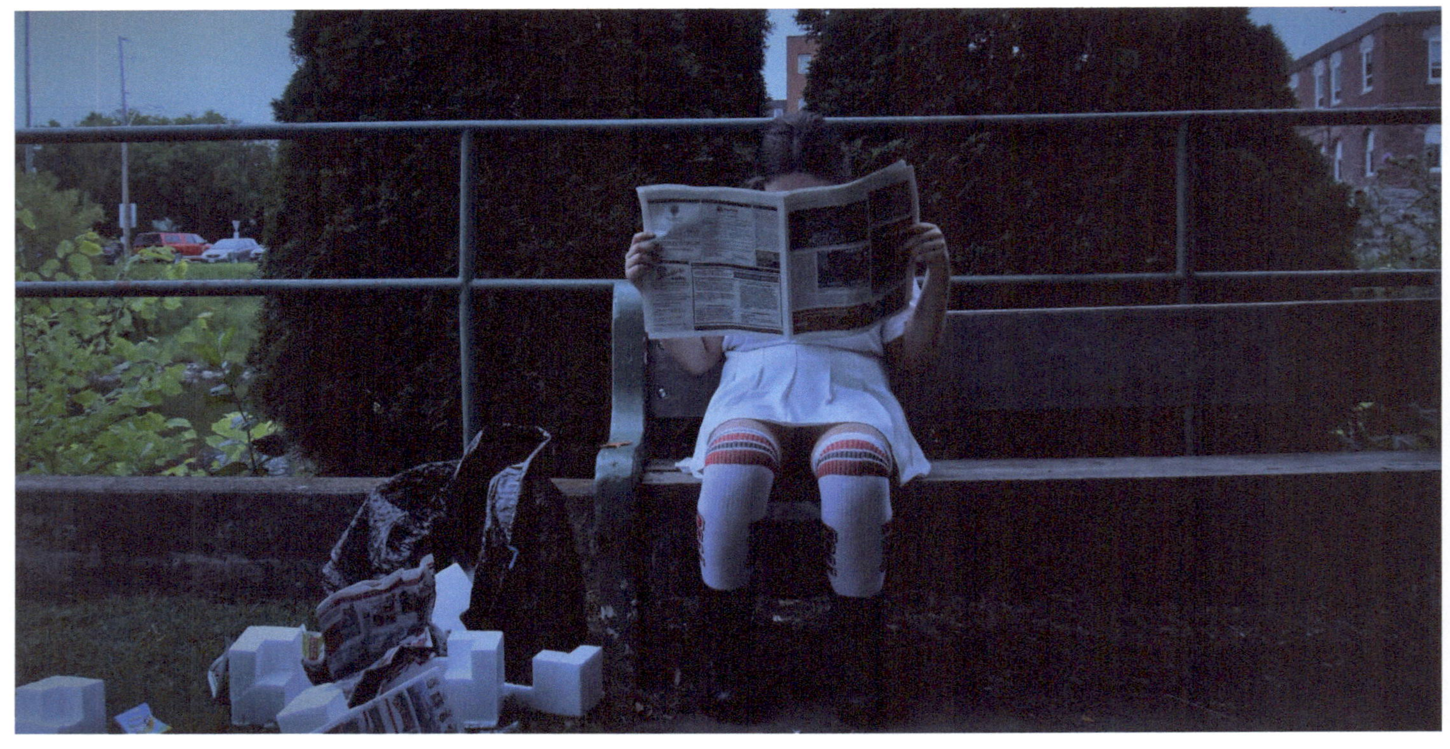

Avoidance, Øzen, photography, 2021. Model: Emma Pinto.

Avoidance
by ØZEN

This photo depicts a person casually reading a newspaper, presumably ignoring the garbage directly beside them. This piece is implying that people are normalizing, and avoiding the litter and pollution brought into the environment, by we humans. A potential reason we avoid this is due to the overwhelming amount of the garbage surrounding us on a daily basis, parallel to the overwhelm of dealing with it.

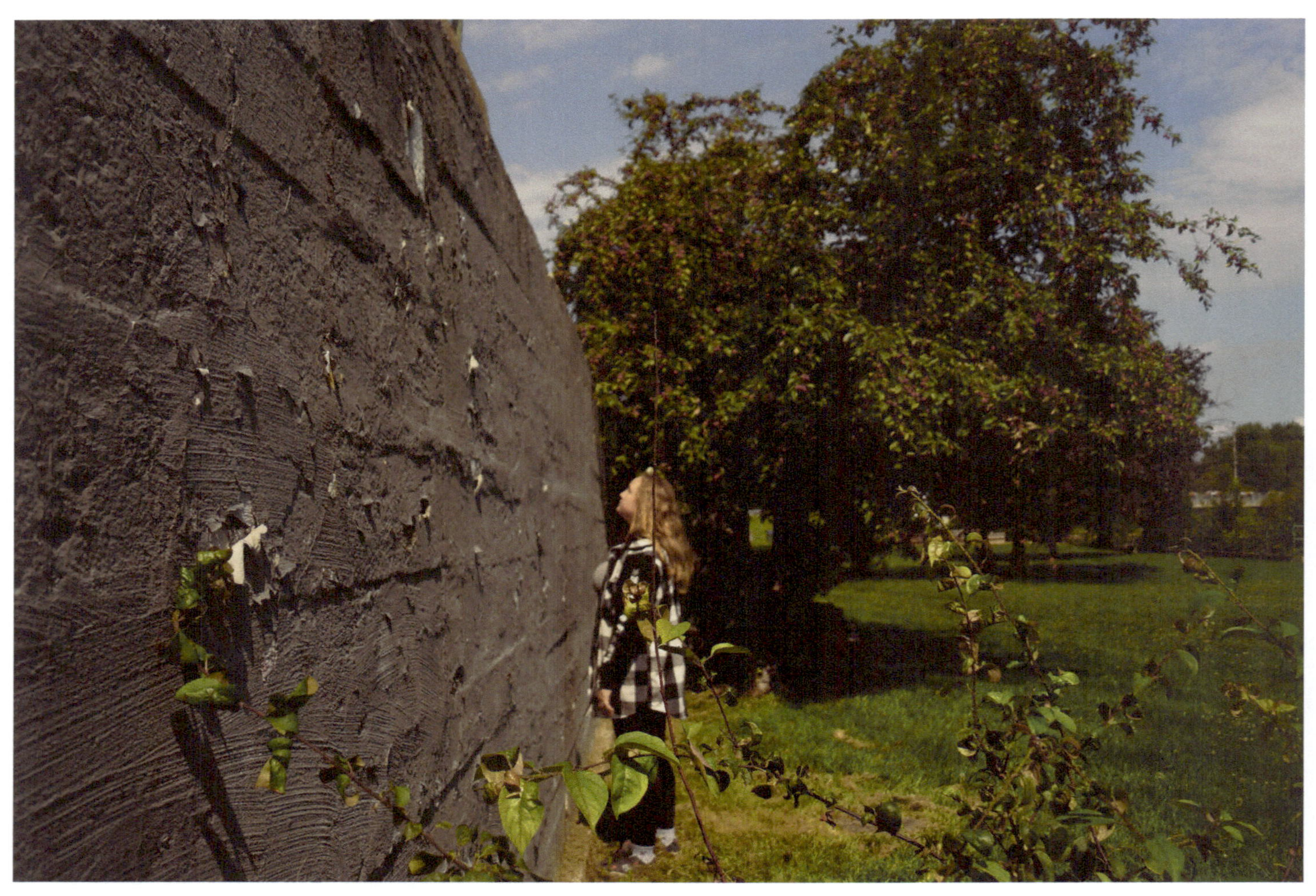

Wall, Emery Verch, photography, 2021. Model: Lindsay St.Amour.

Wall

by Emery Verch

The photo depicts a child staring into a concrete wall. It describes the end of nature itself and how the world is being filled with concrete walls and less trees while people sit and watch. Children need to do something about the environment.

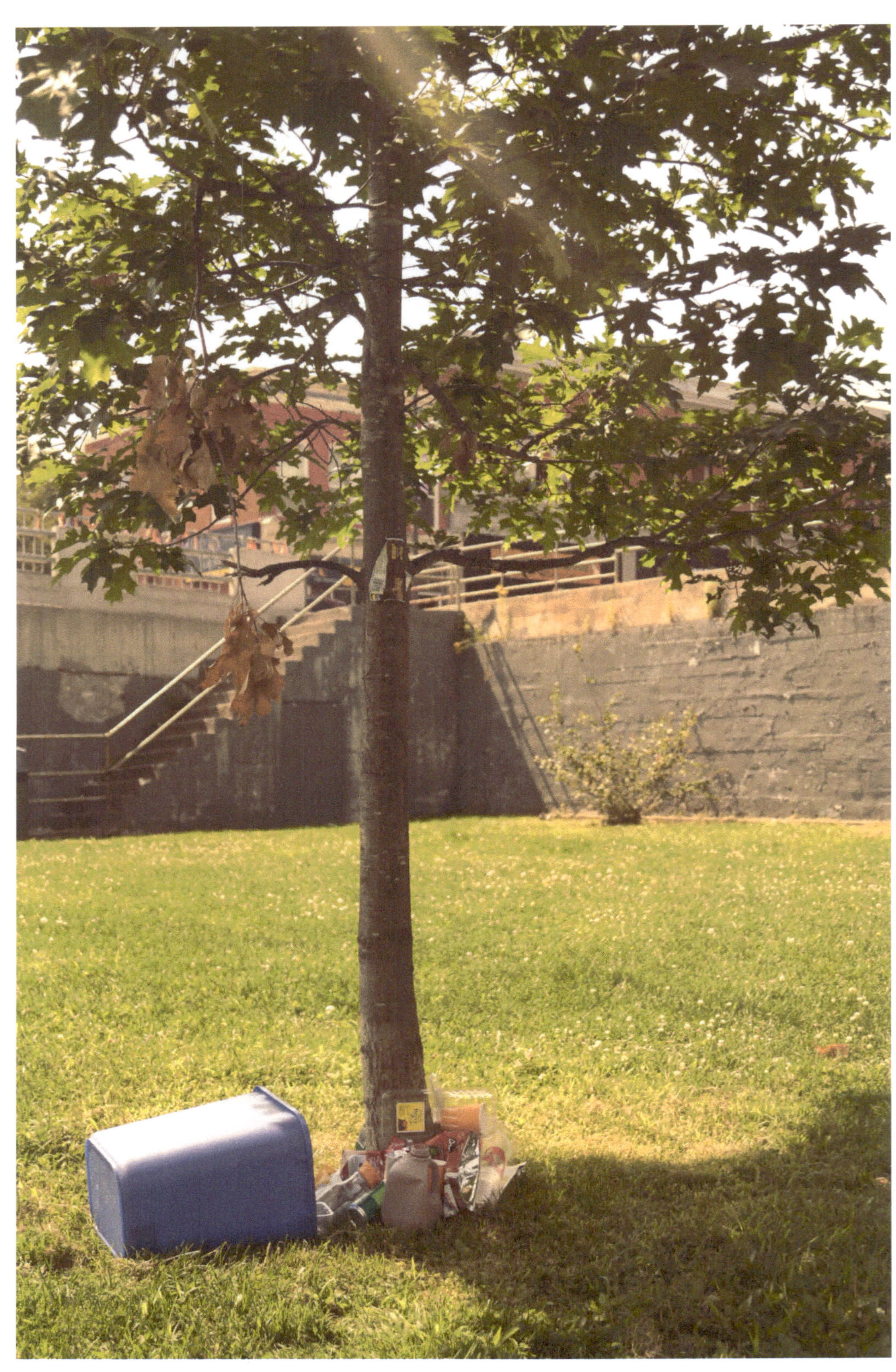

Tree, Lindsay St.Amour, photography, 2021.

Tree
by Lindsay St.Amour

This picture shows how trees are slowly being suffocated. With industrialization, development and pollution the trees are slowly being cut down and disappearing until one day we'll be left with none. Trees are a sustainable resource which need to be replanted. We need to start properly recycling and reusing what we can before we cannot go back.

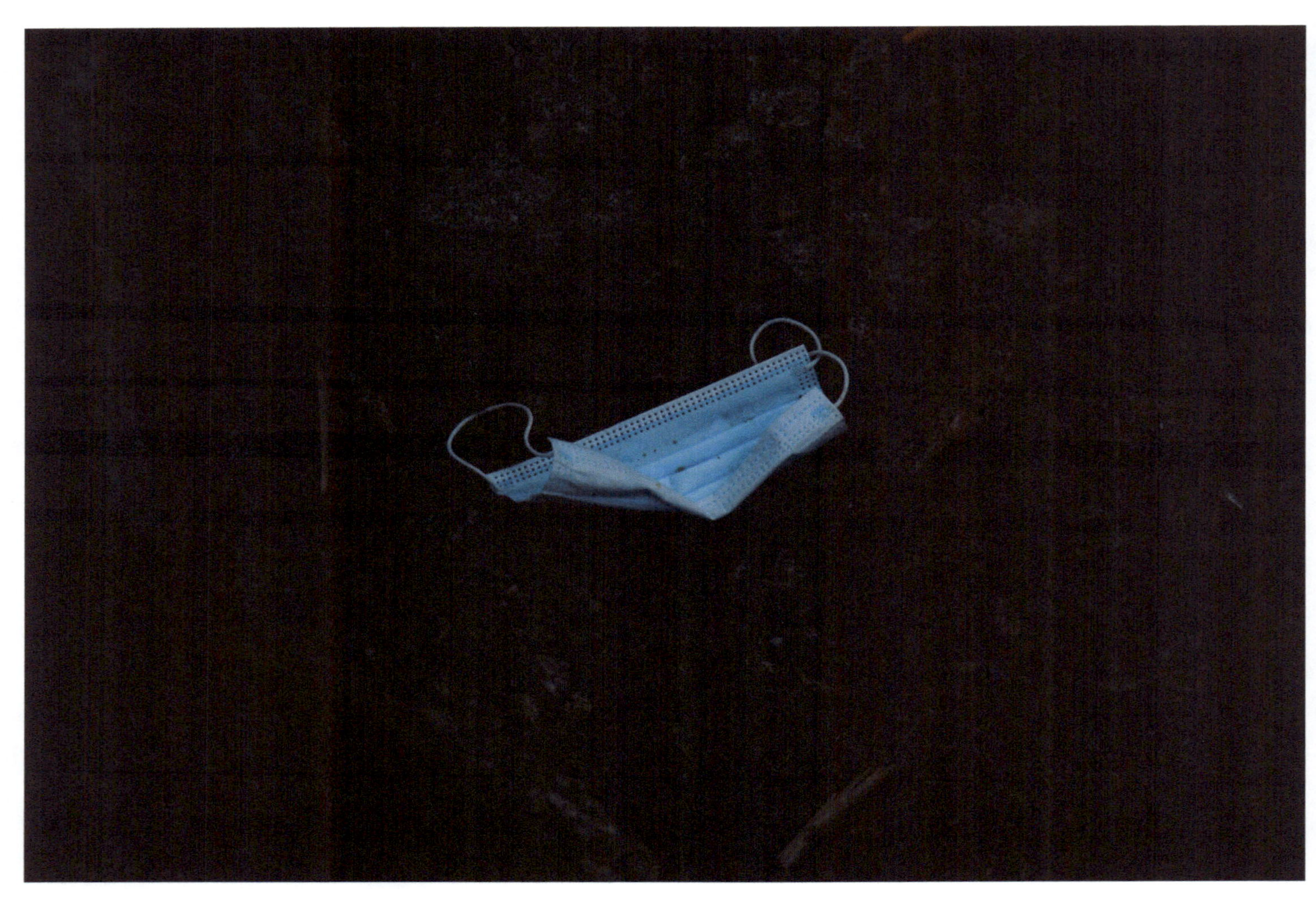

Disposable, Ainsley O'Hagan, photography, 2021.

Disposable
by Ainsley O'Hagan

Over the years this might be something a lot have noticed
Everything becoming 'disposable'.
It started with more and more things made of cheap plastic to cut costs
and raise profits.
Pots and pans no longer lasting like before.
Disposable
A.K.A. it's easier to buy a new one every time it's worn
It's torn,
It breaks,
It cracks.
Because it's disposable right?
You don't have to put a little time into repairing it or washing it or sewing
it shut.
Our disposable culture will end us
Unless we change

Then, the pandemic came
And with the pandemic came masks...
Disposable masks....
Masks...
An item masking our planet every time they get trashed.

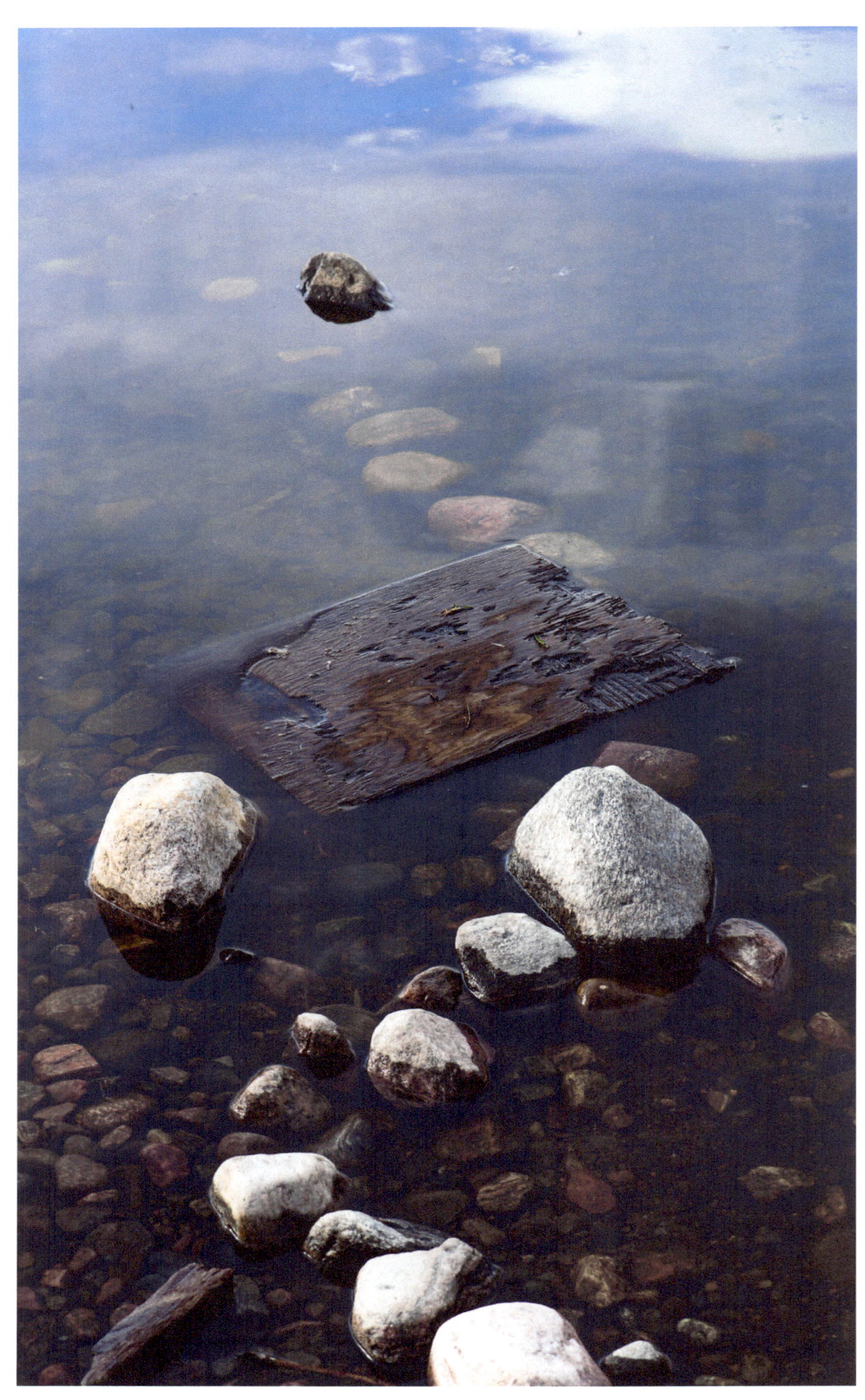

Interruption, Rose Bennett, photography, 2021.

Interruption

by Rose Bennett

Following the natural flow of rocks into the water
Only to be stopped in your tracks by discarded trash.
The combination of trash and waterways
Has become familiar to us.
We need to get back to trash being unusual
And not integrated into our landscape.

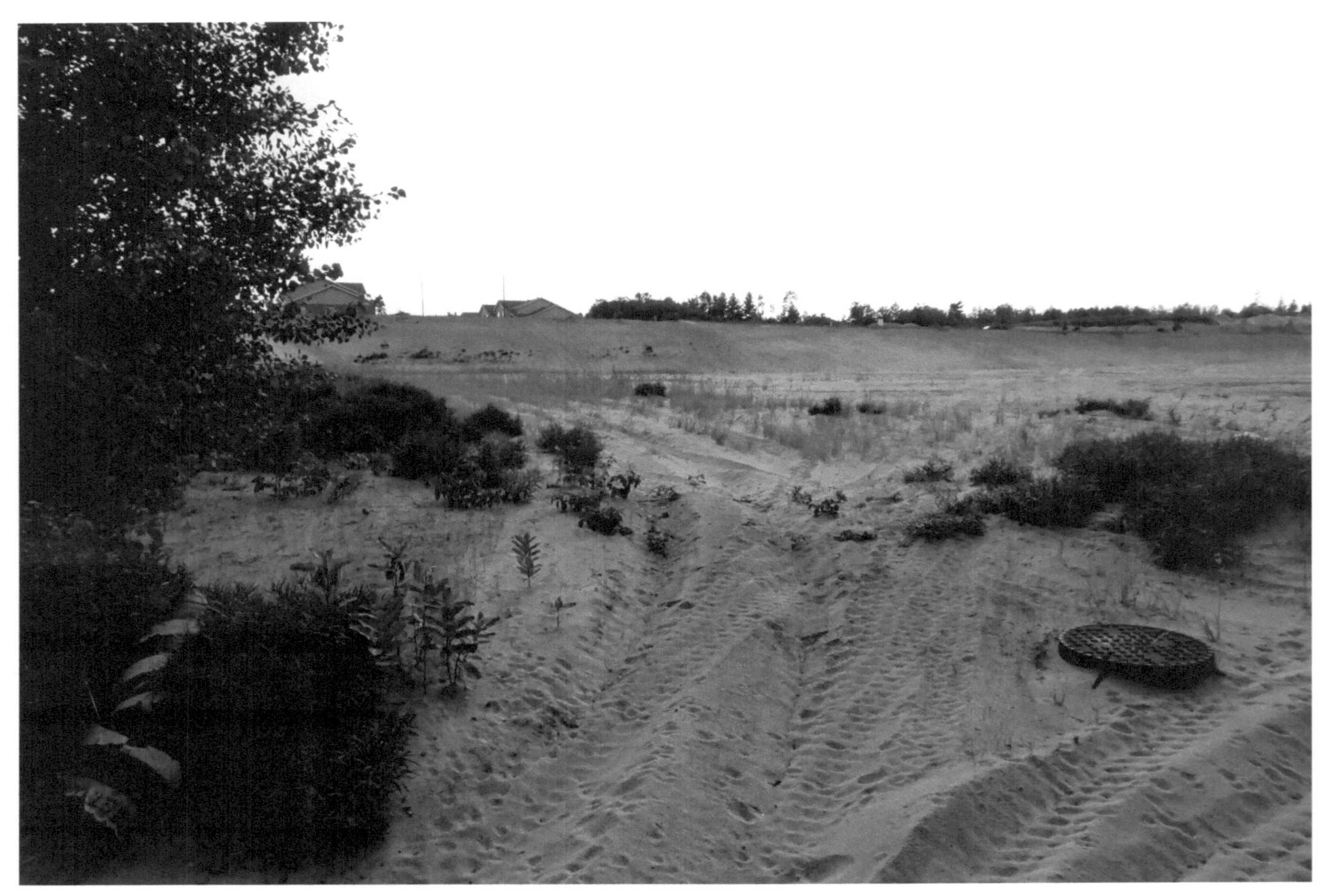

Destructive Sand Dune, Hilda Young, photography, 2021.

Destructive Sand Dune

by Hilda Young

Development... progress?
Commercial reality?
Man Made
& waiting...

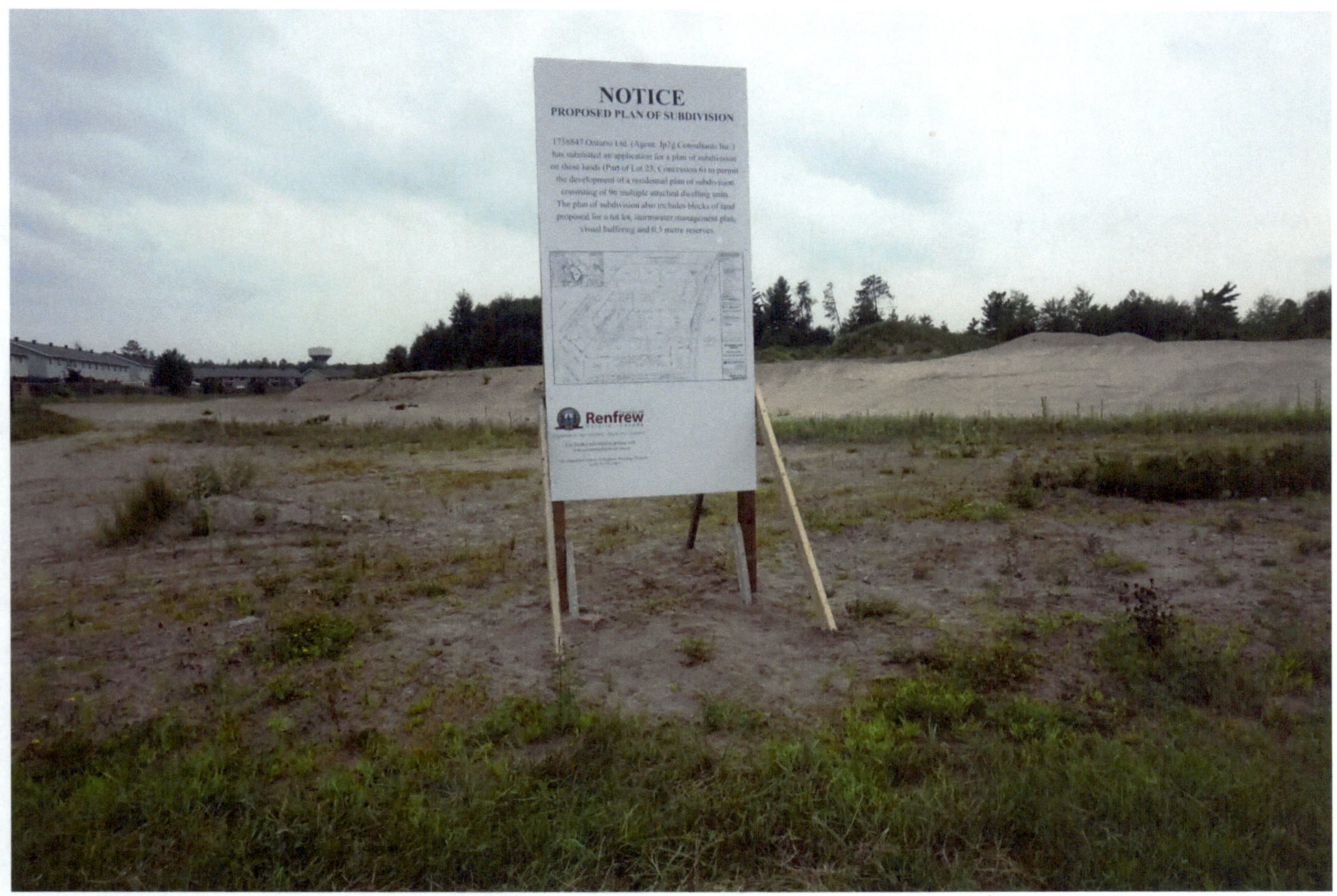

Planning, Hilda Young, photography, 2021.

At this point in time, I am angry that the Town of Petawawa has allowed the developers to clear cut the land leaving sand dunes, and has not enforced nor suggested any type of cover such as sod to protect the sand. It is an eyesore for the community. The change suggested would be an active group of environmentalists lobbying the town to enact bylaws stating that the developer has to develop the land within a certain period of time, and if the development does not happen on time, the town can change the zoning and get better use of the land. The town had a chance when it was formed in the 1990s to plan an attractive community. Instead they left it at the hands of business, and this is the result.

by Hilda Young

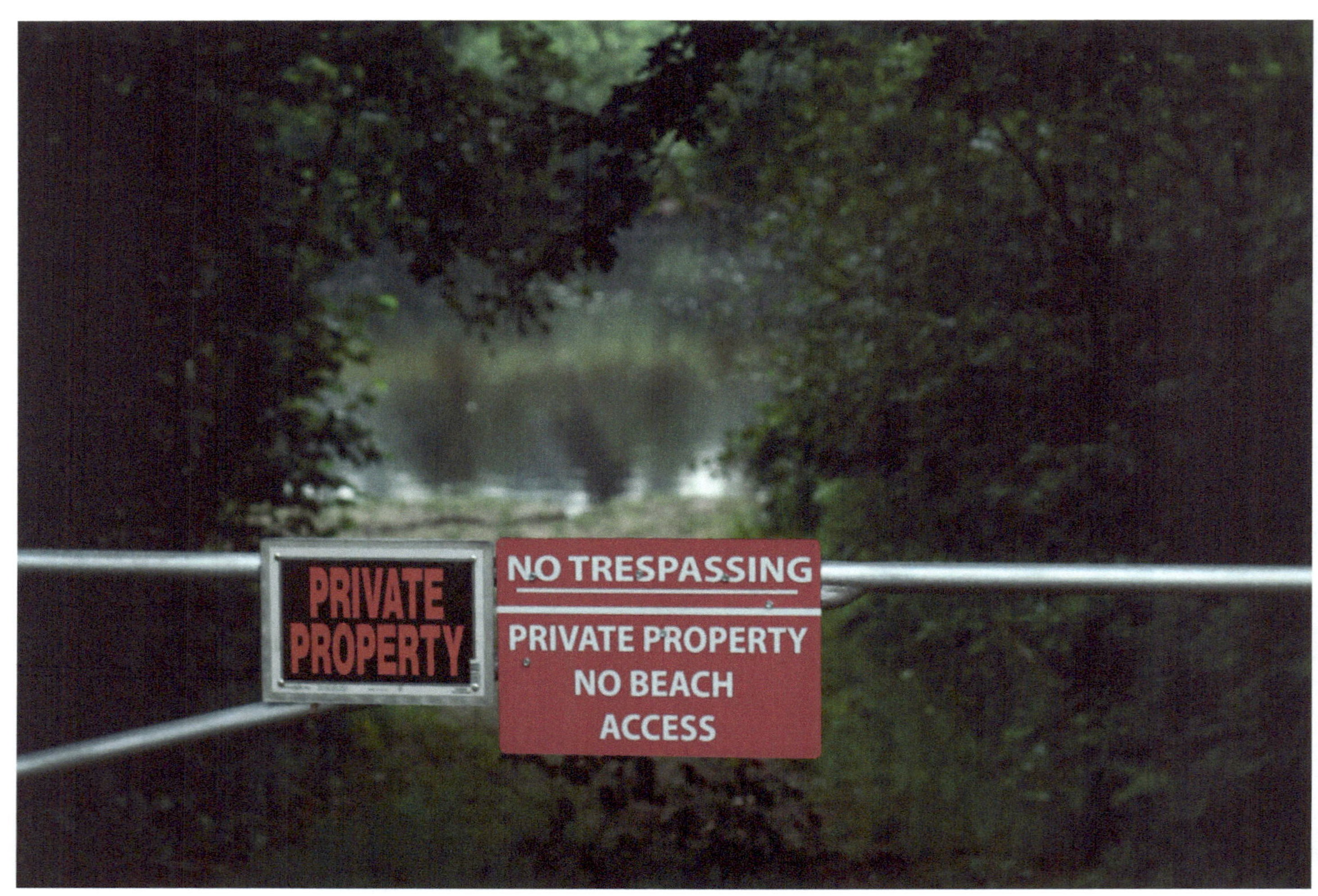

No Trespassing, Tys Burger, photography, 2021.

No Trespassing
by Tys Burger

This is a picture of a beach where I swam for many years with my friends. It is on the Black River in Quebec. The area has seen a lot of development in the past few years and this beach got sold and decorated with a metal barrier and a bunch of 'no trespassing' signs—there are 9 signs in total in the immediate area.

Though the link is a bit abstracted in this example, it is my belief that private property is at the core of the climate change issue. Before the arrival of Europeans on North American land, The First Nations lived in communal societies and did not share our idea of 'ownership' of land—how absurd that concept really is, to own something that is constantly changing, that was here before us, and will be here long after us. The idea of 'my land', enables us to do whatever we want with the land: work it until it's nutrients are depleted, mine every mineral or drop of petroleum, cut down every tree, banish animals from their homes. My hope is that this project will encourage you to think about property differently, and consider communal relationships to land, and take some lessons from the people that were living here before us.

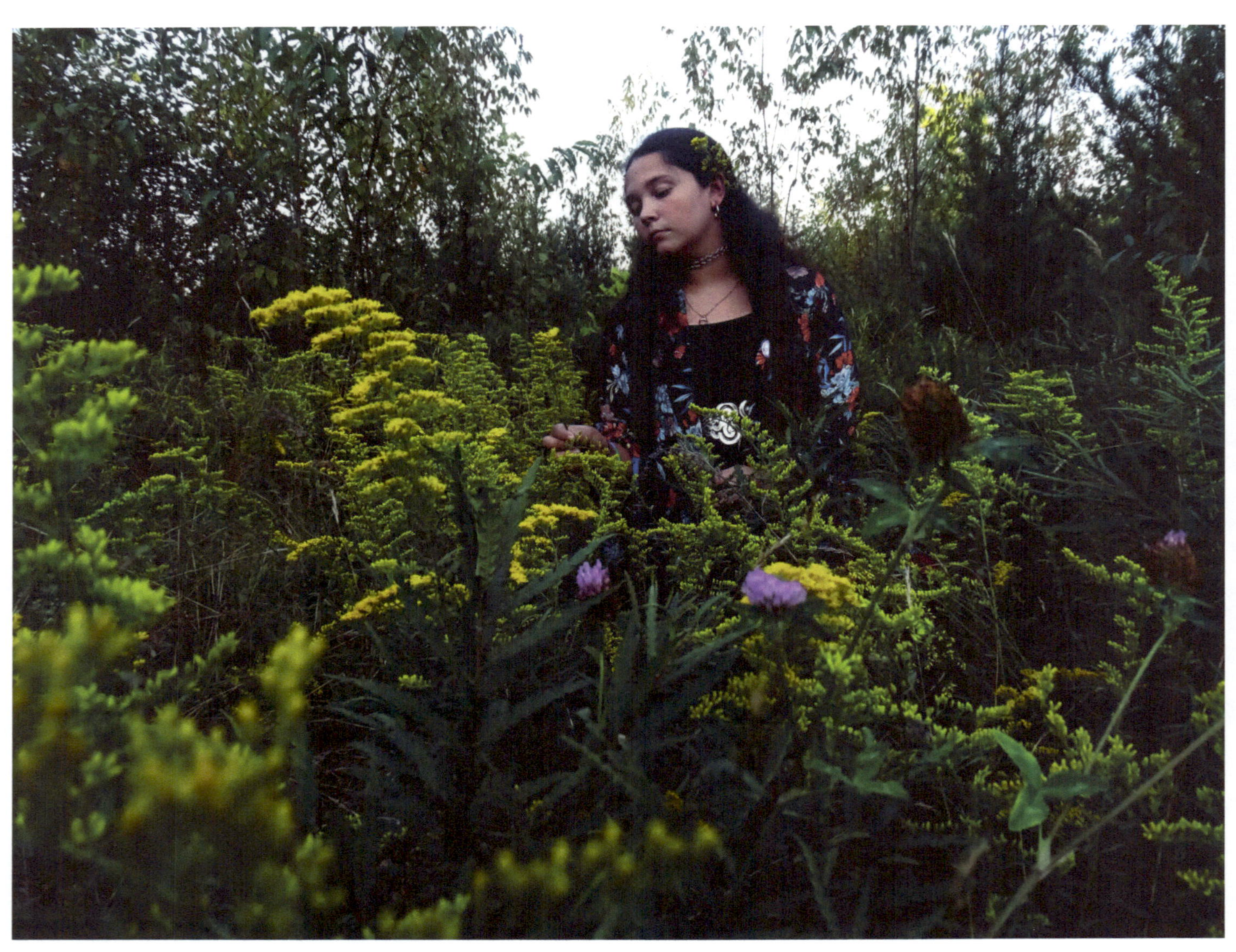

One Last Walk in the Forest on Violet Street, Clare Leamen, photography, 2021.
Model: Brenna Leamen.

One Last Walk in the Forest on Violet Street

by Clare Leamen

"Want to go down to the forest on Violet Street?"
My sister and I love to play in this forest by our house. It holds special childhood memories. I am happy and nostalgic there.
The forest was sold to developers and now it will be cut down.

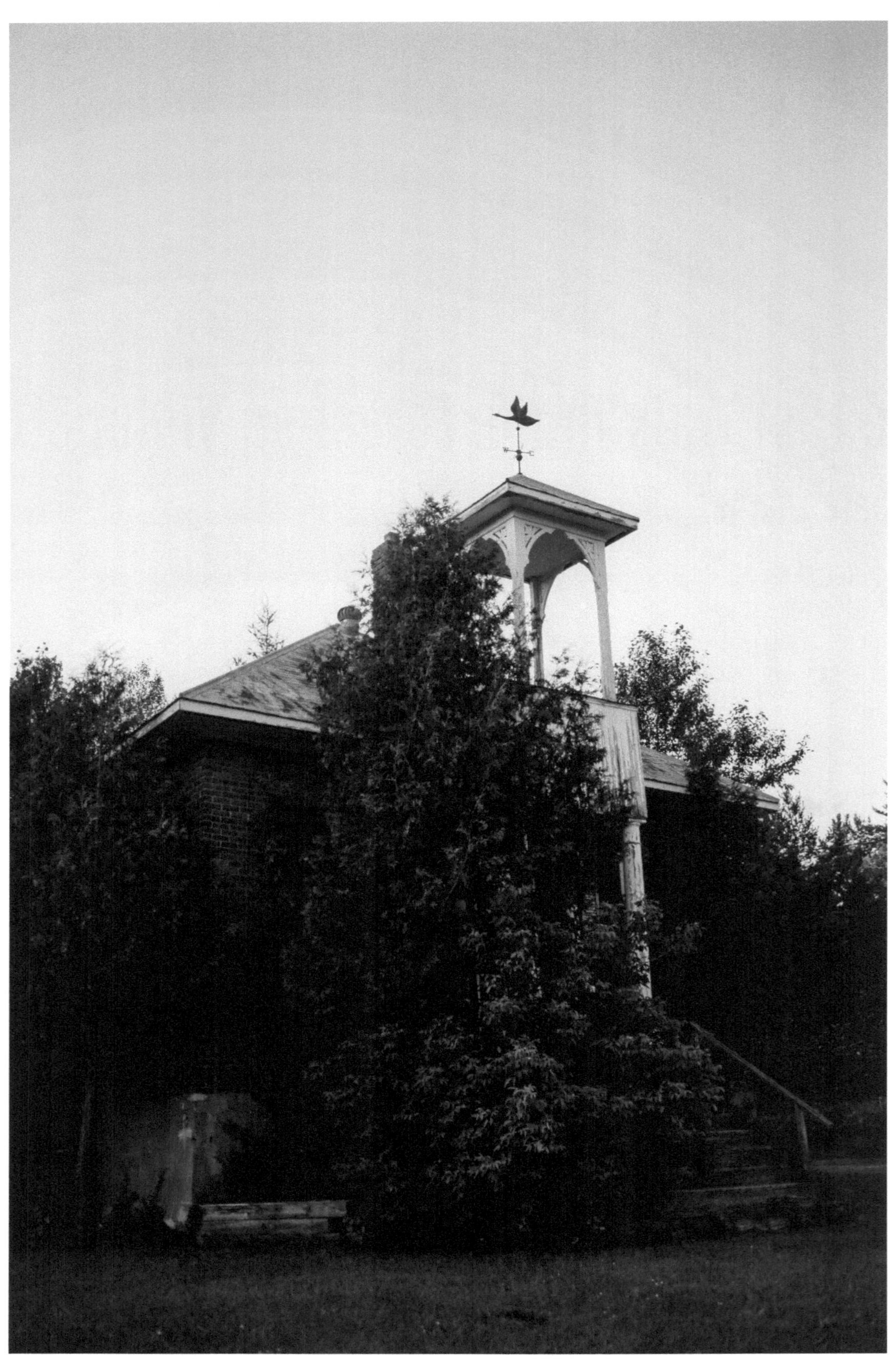

Taking it Back, Caroline Rex, photography, 2021.

Taking it Back
by Caroline Rex

The photo shows a building with trees and plants coming out of it. It represents the fact that, regardless of our response to global warming and environmental disasters, nature will always reclaim what is rightfully theirs. We can either work alongside nature, fixing our mistakes & making things right, or continue on the route we're on, working against it and face the consequences of living with nature that is taking back their home.

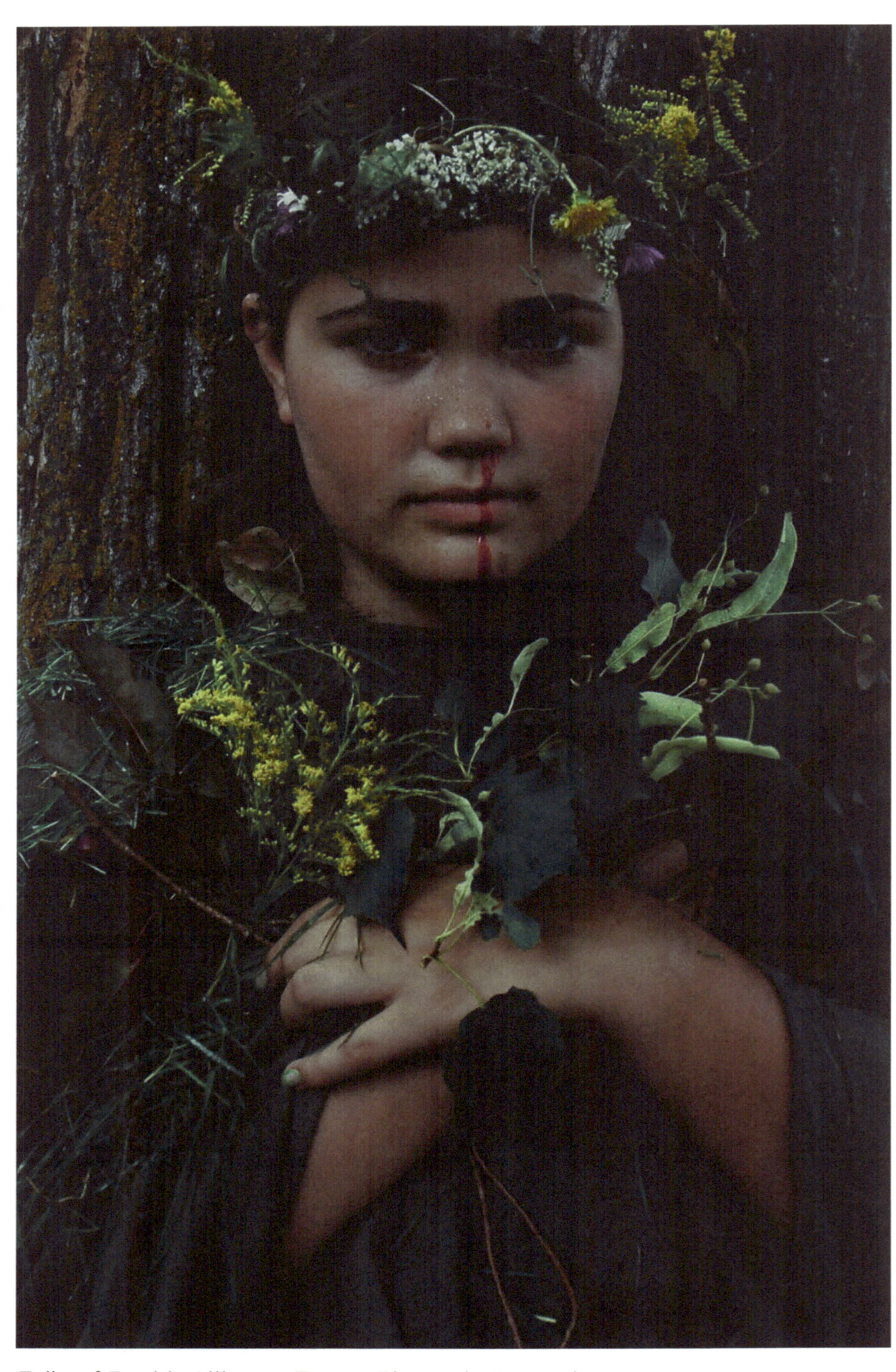

Exile of Earthly Alliance, Emma Pinto, photography, 2021.
Model: Emery Verch.

Exile of Earthly Alliance
by Emma Pinto

This photo represents the destruction of our home planet,
The chaos and pain we've caused.
It feels almost as if Mother Earth herself is calling for help;
As more blood drips, more time is wasted.
We need to act now to make sure the vibrant land
We had before
Isn't lost to a distant memory.

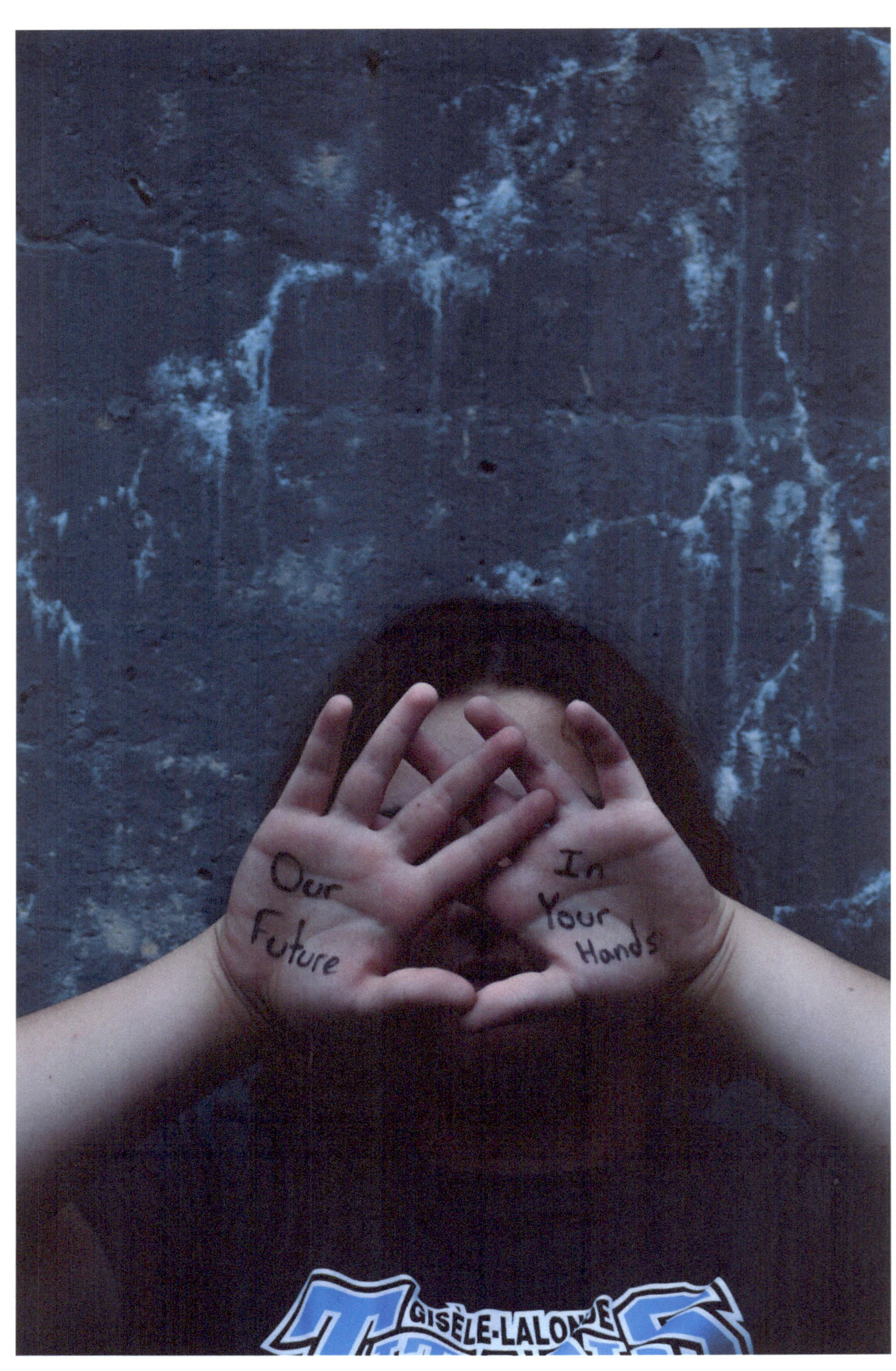

Our Future is in Your Hands, Ki Myra, photography, 2021.
Model: Ainsley O'Hagan.

Our Future is in Your Hands
by Ki Myra

This piece represents the horrid reality of climate change and how it is affecting the economy. It destroys and it conquers, and without your help a barren, boiling wasteland will be our normal. "Our future is in your hands" means exactly that. The future will be nothing but horror, unless you say something about it.

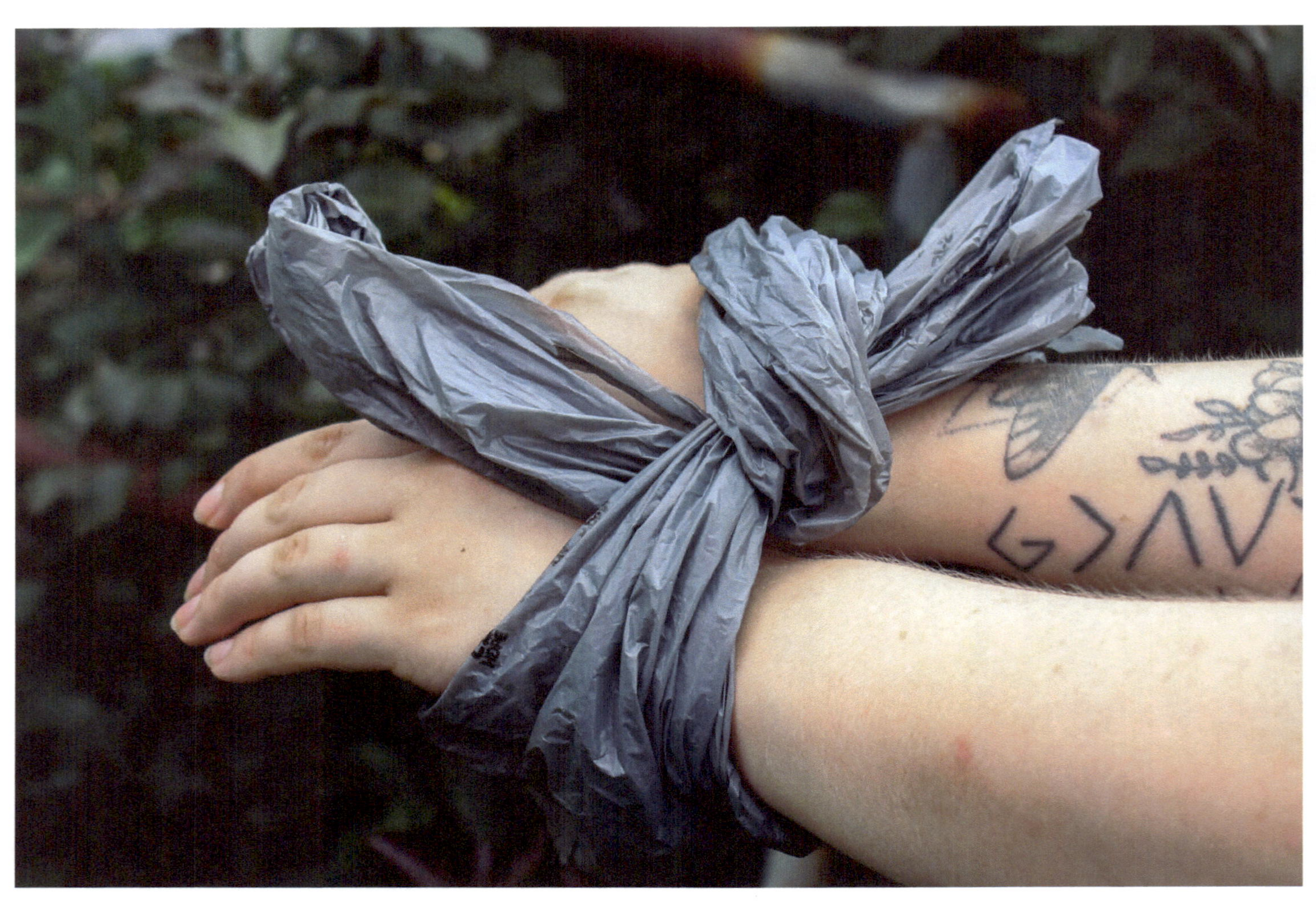

Tied Up Future, Meara Caughey, photography, 2021. Model: Caroline Rex.

Tied Up Future

by Meara Caughey

This piece showcases how our future is tied up because of the choices we, humanity, have made. Not necessarily me, or you, as individual people, but the choices of corporations and governments who have neglected and ignored this issue, who have continued to dump toxic waste into our oceans, who have polluted our air, who have made us feel helpless against this worldwide emergency. Only we have the power to change the future. If we don't start soon, our hands will be tied up, and our planet will be destroyed.

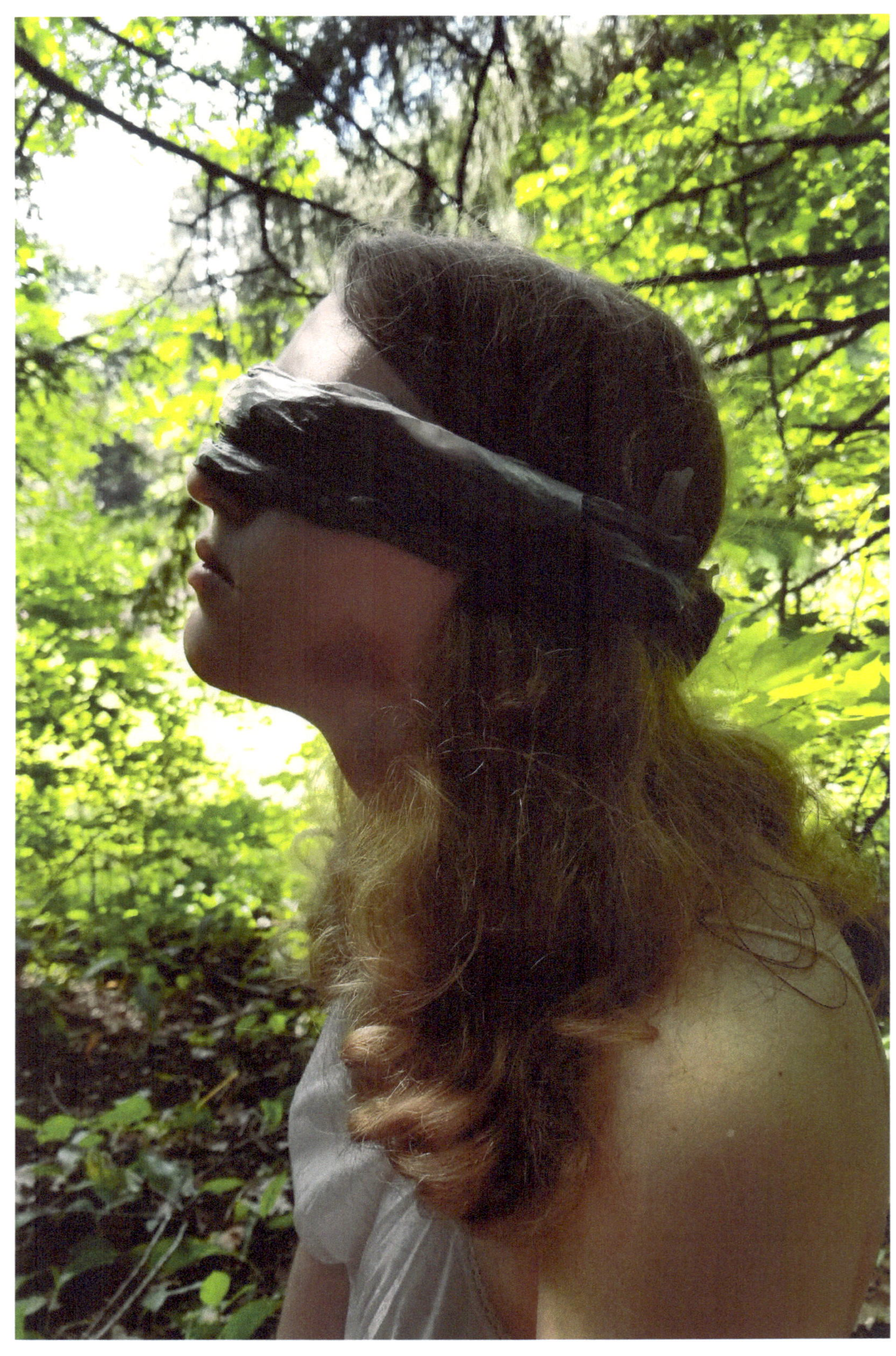

Helpless, Argo Jackson-Beek, photography, 2021. Model: Melody

Helpless

by Argo Jackson-Beek

Sometimes I dream about someone drowning and there is nothing I can do to save them. That is how I feel as I watch nature getting destroyed. I feel disappointment in the human race. <u>We</u> are doing this to the planet. We need to change and we are running out of time.

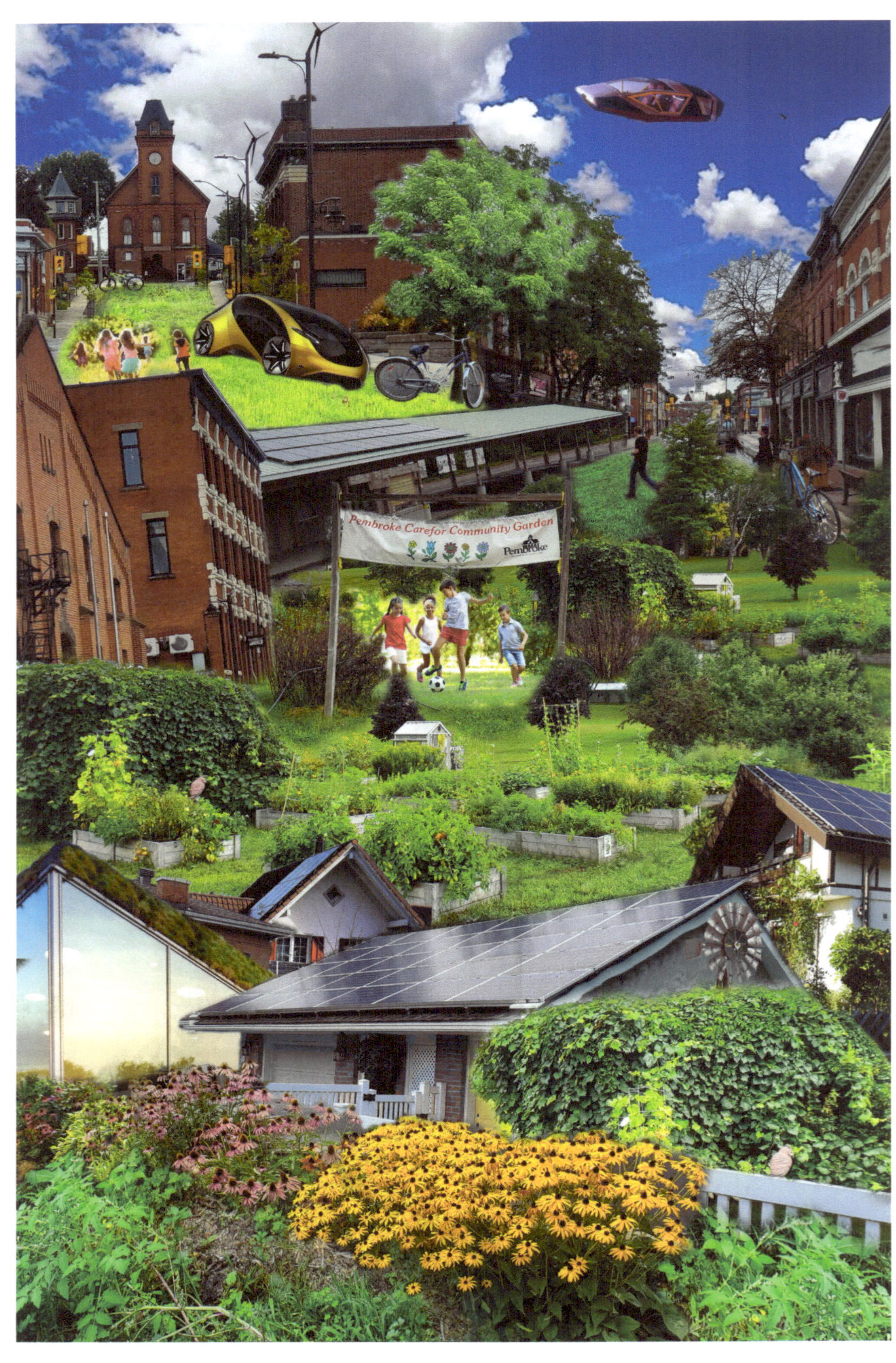

Visions of My Community's Future, Cameron (Dreamshare) Montgomery,
photography collage, 2021.

Visions of My Community's Future
by Cameron (Dreamshare) Montgomery

Very often, pop culture depictions of the future are bleak and dystopian. The Earth is City Planet, Her entire surface covered with grey buildings, digital screens and trash. I love the Solarpunk aesthetic because it helps us to imagine a different future for ourselves, one that challenges our collective intelligence and compassion to use our brains to create green solutions to environmental crises. I often create art about speculative future cities, but this one is about my own home, the town I grew up in. The vision in this piece is just as possible as City Planet if we work together to make it so. Addressing climate destruction starts right here at home. What steps will you take in your own life and community to do better for our future?